Scary Creatures OF THE CITY

Written by
Penny Clarke

Created and designed
by David Salariya

BOOK HOUSE

Author:

Penny Clarke is an author and editor specialising in information books for children. She has written titles on natural history, rainforests and volcanoes, as well as others on different periods of history. She used to live in central London, but thanks to modern technology she has now realised her dream of being able to live and work in the countryside.

Artists:
Janet Baker & Julian Baker
(JB Illustrations)
Robert Morton
Nick Hewetson
David Antram
John James

Series Creator:

David Salariya was born in Dundee, Scotland. He established The Salariya Book Company in 1989. He has illustrated a wide range of books and has created many new series for publishers in the UK and overseas. He lives in Brighton with his wife, illustrator Shirley Willis, and their son.

Editorial Assistants:
Rob Walker, Tanya Kant

Picture Research:
Mark Bergin

Photo Credits:

t=top, b=bottom

Dreamstime: 7, 15b, 18, 27, 29
Fotolia: 8, 9, 19
iStockphoto: 6, 10, 11, 15t, 17, 25, 26
Mark Bergin: 12

Published in Great Britain in 2009 by
Book House, an imprint of
The Salariya Book Company Ltd
25 Marlborough Place, Brighton BN1 1UB

SALARIYA

A catalogue record for this book is available from the British Library.

HB ISBN: 978-1-906370-83-1
PB ISBN: 978-1-906370-84-8

Printed in China

Contents

American alligator

What's a scary creature?

A scary creature is any animal, whatever its size, that is a danger to humans or is feared by them. All over the world, more people now live in cities than in the countryside. As cities grow, wild creatures have less space in which to live. Some compete with humans for space in the countryside. Others move into cities.

Why are these animals scary?

Is it because they're fierce? Because they hunt in packs or at night? Because they occur in large numbers? Or because they're wild?

In India and Vietnam, some monkeys have adapted so well to city living that they have become serious pests.

Langur monkey

Raccoon

Raccoons and snapping turtles have colonised suburbs in Canada and the United States.

Mouse

Rat

Rats and mice thrive on scraps of waste food thrown away by humans. Fewer humans would mean fewer rats and mice!

Snapping turtle

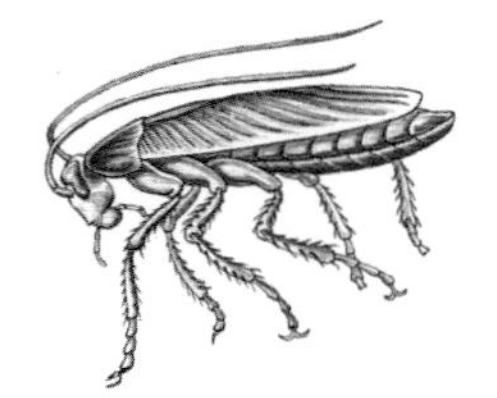

Cockroach

Fly

Flea

Insects such as flies, fleas and cockroaches can infest human homes very quickly, especially where there is waste. Fleas and cockroaches are difficult to deal with because they are small and can easily hide behind cupboards and in soft furnishings.

Why do cities attract scary creatures?

Because there is food! Humans, especially in the developed world, are wasteful. Next time you are in the school playground or a busy shopping street, look at all the discarded food: partly eaten burgers and pizzas, sandwiches and crisps. It may be rubbish to us, but it's food to many other living things.

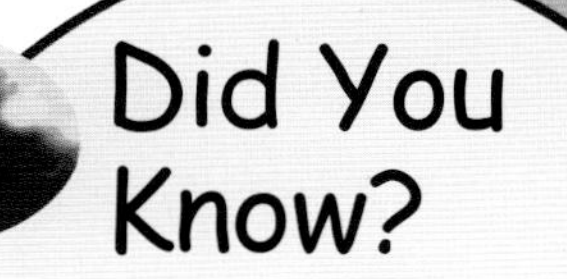

Did You Know?

Polar bears are good swimmers, but because there is now less ice in the Arctic they have to travel further between **ice floes**. This can be dangerous – if their fur becomes waterlogged, they may drown.

The melting Arctic ice sheet makes hunting harder for polar bears. These scary animals have learnt that rubbish bins in human settlements make good food sources.

Polar bear in downtown Vancouver, Canada

Monkeys are pests in many cities in India and Nepal. At first they raided outlying farms and gardens. Now they live in city centres, stealing from markets, entering homes and even attacking people. Hinduism, India's official religion, does not allow the killing of animals. Instead, city officials try to round up the monkeys and **sterilise** them. But how easy is it to catch a monkey?

Rhesus monkey inside a temple in Nepal

Langur monkeys in the grounds of a temple in Agra, India

What happens to our rubbish bins?

Throughout the developed world, animals have learnt that cities provide easy living. Raccoons, foxes and coyotes used to come out only at night. The only evidence of their existence in cities was finding overturned rubbish bins in the morning. Now many of these new city-dwellers are so bold that you may well see them during the day.

Raccoon inside a rubbish bin

Did You Know?

Raccoons, foxes and coyotes are **scavengers**: they eat all sorts of things that other animals leave behind. That is why they have adapted so successfully to city life.

City streets often have few trees and no undergrowth, but there are parks, gardens and other places for resourceful creatures to hide by day. Then, at night, they come out to feed: raccoons in the Americas, and rats and mice everywhere in the world.

Raccoons are mainly **nocturnal** (night-time) animals, but they do occasionally venture out in the day. They are good climbers and spend the day hidden in trees or bushy undergrowth.

Is it only food that they want?

No – most living things need water as well. In Australia, the 'Big Dry' – the severe drought in the south-east that began in 2003 – is forcing creatures that normally avoid humans to venture into townships in search of food and water. Dingoes (Australian wild dogs) are shy animals, but they are now coming into town because rivers have dried up, and their usual **prey** of rabbits and kangaroos is dying off.

A dingo stealing food from the back of a trailer

Did You Know?

Water is more important for survival than food. **Dehydration** (lack of water or other liquid) kills more quickly than **starvation** (lack of food).

The 'Big Dry' has killed off the plants and insects that emus eat. Now these scarily large birds – up to 2 metres tall – are coming into towns.

Are habitats in danger?

Yes. Modern technologies like central heating and air-conditioning enable humans to live in places that were not suitable for them fifty years ago. When humans start to take over animal **habitats**, the habitats change and often become unlivable for the wild animals.

The Everglades, Florida, USA

Once there were only wild animals here, including dangerous alligators and mosquitoes. Now there are tourist boats and even houses.

Alligator in the Everglades

NO SWIMMING

Are the Everglades changing?

Yes – nowadays, homes can be built on swampy ground, **insecticides** can get rid of mosquitoes, and it's easy to enlarge the Everglades' natural waterways for leisure craft. And so human incomers displace the original wild inhabitants of this unique and fragile habitat.

Humans may have moved in, but, as the sign above shows, scary creatures still lurk in the habitat that was once their own.

Snapping turtles are aggressive **carnivores**. They get their name from the way they snap their powerful jaws shut on their prey: fish, frogs or water birds.

Snapping turtle

Why are disasters good for scavengers?

Disasters such as earthquakes, floods and fires leave behind the dead bodies of humans and animals. These provide food for many scary scavengers. Scavenging is nature's way of preventing disease, but in today's densely populated world it brings people and animals into conflict.

Clearing up after disasters must be swift – otherwise deadly diseases such as cholera and typhoid will occur.

Following a hurricane, huge waves can cause enormous damage.

Plague of locusts in ancient Egypt

What are plagues?

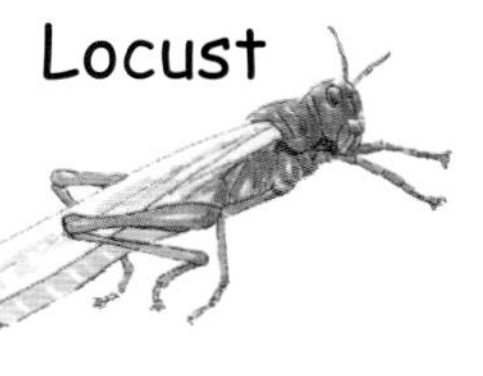

Locust

Colorado beetle

Mosquito

When an animal or insect population suddenly grows unusually large, it is called a plague. Plagues of locusts, which are described in ancient texts, still do enormous damage to crops in parts of Africa. Large swarms of Colorado beetles can destroy potato crops. Mosquitoes spread diseases such as malaria.

How do scavengers help?

Scavengers speed up the process of decay. Flies lay their eggs in the dead creature's flesh so that the maggots that hatch have a ready supply of food. Hyenas and vultures, which can smell a **carcass** many miles away, come to pick the bones clean of flesh. The sooner the flesh is removed, the less risk there is of spreading disease.

Vultures and hyena feeding on a carcass

Why do we need clean water?

Drinking water **contaminated** with **bacteria** causes outbreaks of deadly diseases such as typhoid and cholera, which spread rapidly where people live in crowded conditions. In the 19th century, scientists realised the importance of clean water, and engineers began to design modern sewage and drinking-water systems. Without them, life in today's huge cities would be impossible.

Modern wastewater treatment plant

Freshwater snail

Is it always safe to swim?

Swimming in contaminated pools and rivers can cause serious illnesses. One disease that occurs mainly in developing countries is bilharzia. It is caught from **parasites** called flukes that live on freshwater snails. The flukes' **larvae** can penetrate the skin. Female flukes may lay eggs inside the human body. The disease can damage internal organs.

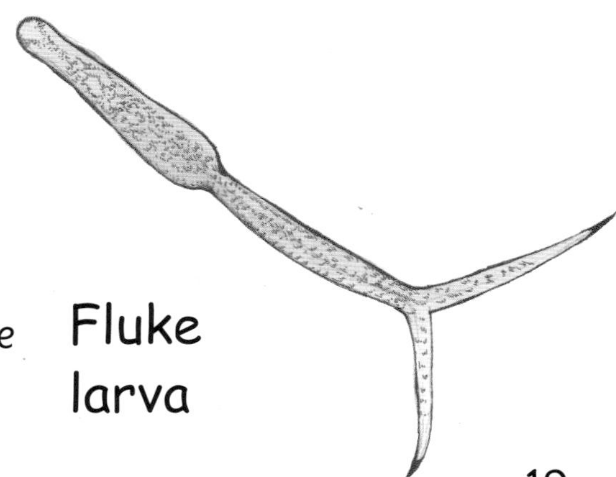

Fluke larva

Surely we're safe at home?

No, not really. Many other **species** find city living just as pleasant as we do. Buildings with central heating and air-conditioning attract all kinds of creatures, from **microscopic** dust mites to large rats. Even escaped pet snakes enjoy the warmth to be found in city buildings – and the ready supply of mice.

X-Ray Vision

Hold the next page up to the light and see what's lurking inside a room!

See what's inside

Flea

What are fleas?

Fleas are blood-sucking insects that spread disease germs when they bite their prey. They cannot fly, but jump from **host** to host. This is why they thrive in crowded places.

Escaped pet python in air-conditioning duct
Bedbugs
Flies
Fleas
Fleas
Cockroaches
Cockroaches
Rats in drains
Mice

What might be in our walls?

All sorts of things you'd probably rather not know about! The picture opposite shows many of the creatures that might be sharing your home. Human dwellings provide them with food and warmth. Their highways are the drains, pipes and ducts within skyscrapers and tower blocks that lead from one food source to the next.

The human body louse looks very like the head louse shown below. The body louse carries typhus and lays its eggs in dirty clothes. Once people understood the importance of clean clothes, the insect became less common.

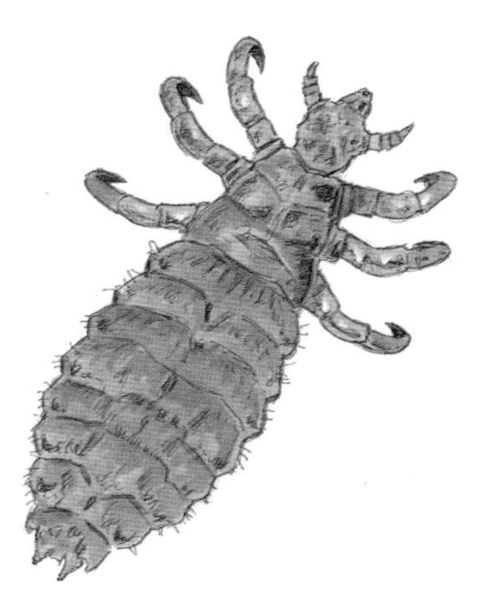

Human head louse

This louse lays its eggs or 'nits' in human hair. The lice live on blood that they get by biting through the scalp, which makes us itch.

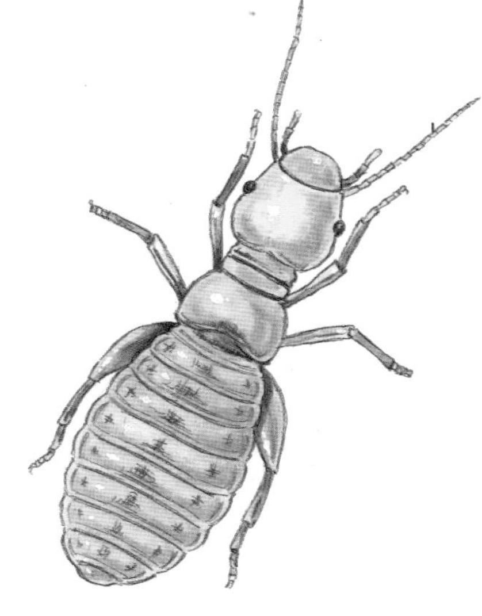

Book louse

Most so-called book lice live among leaves and in birds' nests in the **tropics**. But one species actually feeds on the glue in old book bindings.

Bedbug

These bugs were very common until people realised how important it was to wash regularly and have clean clothes and clean bedding.

Are these scary creatures threatened?

No! The scary creatures in this book thrive in cities and are not likely to die out. One of the most successful is the black rat. Centuries ago it hitched a lift on sailing ships and travelled all over the world, taking with it the fleas which caused bubonic plague.

Early sailing ships were extremely dirty. No-one understood the importance of good **hygiene**, so rats thrived.

Bubonic plague spread fast, causing panic and fear. This print (above) dates from 1665, the last big outbreak in London.

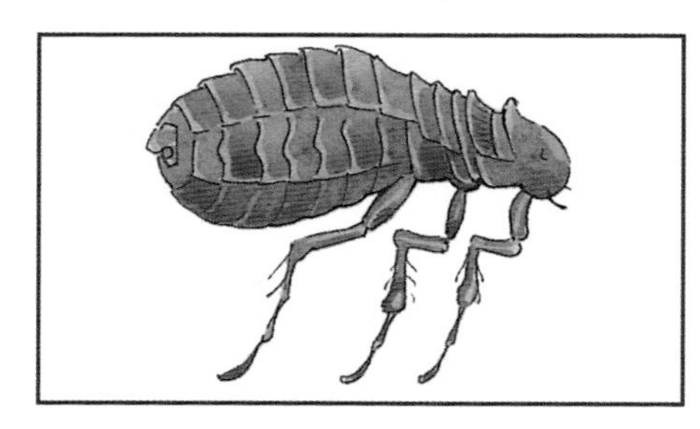

Rat fleas spread the 'Black Death', the bubonic plague that killed about a third of Europe's population in the mid-14th century.

Rats are very agile. They clambered over water barrels and sacks of food, contaminating them with urine and droppings.

Did You Know?

As cities slowly became cleaner, healthier places for humans, they became less attractive to rats and outbreaks of the plague declined.

After dark, bodies were left outside the house in which they'd died, ready to be collected and carted away.

So many people died of the plague that the disposal of their bodies was a major problem.

Modern supermouse

Mice are just as successful as rats, their larger cousins. Much of the food we eat has spent time in huge cold stores. Some mice can now live in these cold stores, having grown thicker coats to protect them from the low temperatures.

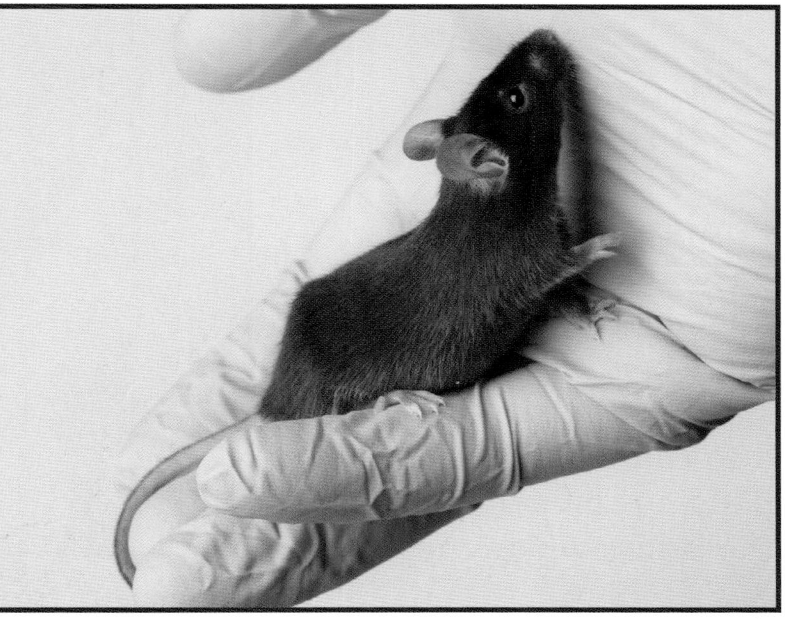

Are these scary creatures a threat to us?

Yes, and they always have been. Many scary creatures have lived alongside humans throughout history: **archaeologists** have found the remains of fleas and rats in ancient tombs. Today, as foxes and wild dogs move into towns and cities they bring diseases such as mange and rabies, which pets may catch. Rabies is nearly always fatal to humans if left untreated.

How can pigeons be dangerous?

Psittacosis is a type of **pneumonia** which can kill humans. The pigeons fed by tourists in city squares can carry it. Their droppings can also cause damage to buildings by piling up on the ledges where they roost.

Feeding pigeons

Did You Know?

It is easier for **urban** foxes to find food than their country cousins, so urban vixens (female foxes) have more cubs. Most urban foxes die before they are three years old from diseases caused by parasites.

Meet your neighbour! Urban foxes are so used to humans that sights like this are now common.

Can we overcome these creatures?

Not really – they adapt too quickly. Most rats, for example, are now immune to poison. Sometimes, when we try to overcome a problem, we cause more harm than good. The insecticide DDT, developed in the 1940s, was extremely effective. Unfortunately, it got into the **food chain** and brought birds of prey like the osprey and sparrowhawk to the edge of extinction.

DDT in the food chain

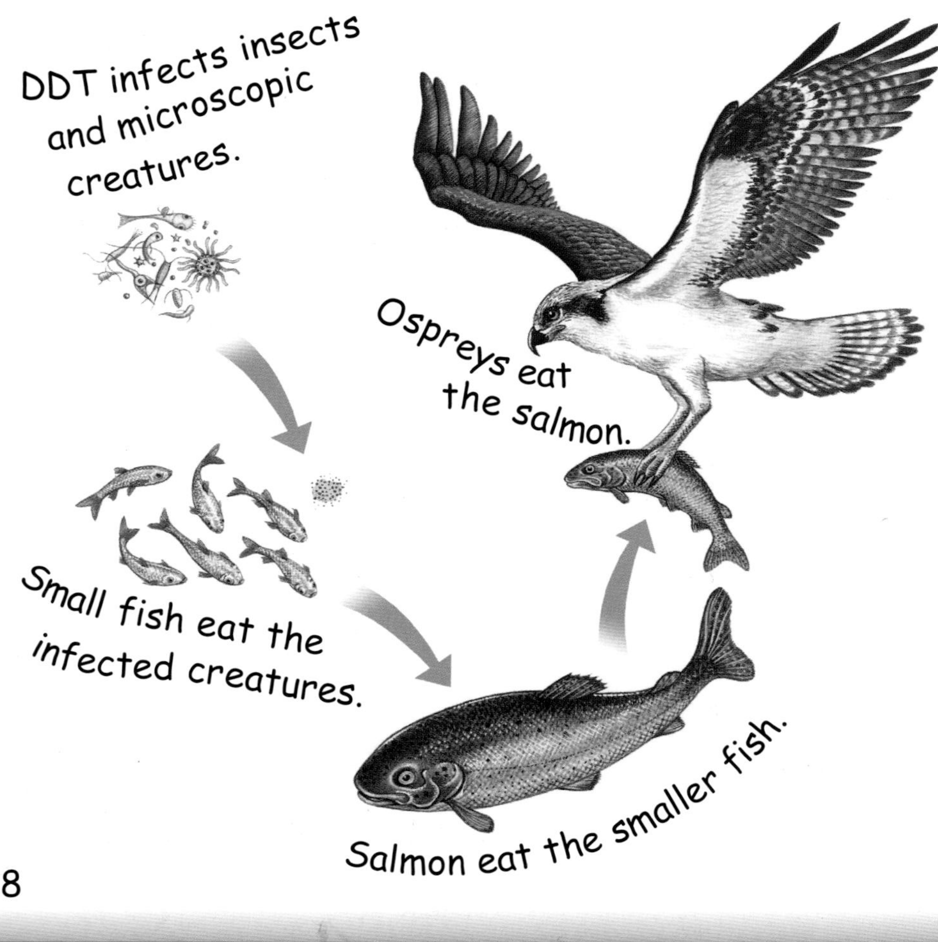

DDT is dangerous because it infects the food chain – the whole series of animals that feed on one another. When it kills insects, the insecticide remains in their bodies. It then passes into the bodies of any creature that eats the insects – and so on up the chain.

Sparrowhawk

Did You Know?

DDT got into the sparrowhawks' bodies when they ate prey contaminated with it. It did not kill the birds, but made the shells of their eggs so thin that few of them hatched.

Malarial mosquitoes

Malaria kills millions of people every year. The disease is carried by the *Anopheles* mosquito, which flourishes in warm countries wherever there is **stagnant water**, from swamps to tiny puddles.

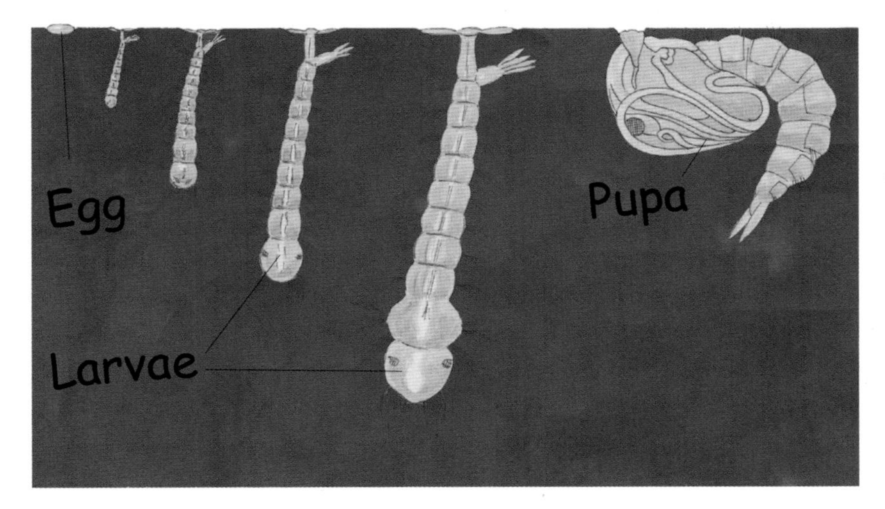

Mosquitoes lay their eggs in water, where the larvae develop into adults. Would it solve the problem if all stagnant water was drained away? No – draining swamps would destroy the habitats of helpful creatures, too.

Female *Anopheles* mosquito

City facts

You don't need harmful chemicals to deal with scary creatures in the home: regular vacuuming kills fleas more efficiently and safely than any chemical. Cockroaches will give your home a miss if there's no food waste lying about.

Each species of mosquito buzzes in a slightly different way, which helps them identify one species from another.

Malaysian schoolchildren learn never to smile at a monkey. Why? A monkey bares its teeth when it is angry. So, naturally, if it sees your teeth it will think you are angry and it may become aggressive in return.

In India the population of the oriental white-backed vulture has fallen by 99% since 1992. A drug used to treat cattle causes kidney failure in vultures that feed on dead cattle.

Polar bears are truly scary. They stand nearly 3 metres tall on their hind legs and can easily outrun a human. Shortage of food is bringing them into northern settlements – and close encounters with humans.

Gulls are a real nuisance in many seaside towns, flying down and grabbing sandwiches and ice-creams from holidaymakers' hands.

A few head lice or nits won't do you much harm. But anyone badly infected with them would feel run-down and not very well. In fact, they would feel 'lousy' – which is where the phrase comes from.

In March 2008 an office block in Bangkok, the capital of Thailand, became infested with rats. Who worked in the offices? The staff of the country's Health Ministry!

In June 2008 flights in and out of Delhi international airport in India came to a standstill. The cause was not a crash, but crowds of jackals, kites and monitor lizards on the runway. June is the rainy season in Delhi. The weather's cool and the ground is sodden. But runways are dry and their hard surfaces radiate warmth – just what the animals needed to help them dry out.

The old saying 'Every cloud has a silver lining' has come true for mosquitoes in Nevada, Arizona and California. Money problems have left many big houses empty, and the water in the unused swimming pools makes wonderful breeding places for mosquitoes. Draining the pools isn't the answer, either – after it rains there's another breeding place for the mosquitoes!

Glossary

archaeologist A scientist who studies the remains left by past civilisations.

bacteria The smallest living things. Some of them can cause diseases.

carcass The dead body of an animal.

carnivore An animal that eats mostly meat.

contaminate To pollute or infect.

dehydration Loss of fluid; losing too much fluid too fast is extremely dangerous.

food chain The series of creatures that feed off one another.

habitat The place where a plant or animal lives naturally.

host A plant or animal on which a parasite lives.

hygiene Keeping clean and healthy.

ice floe A large, thick sheet of floating ice.

insecticide A chemical that kills insects.

larva (plural **larvae**) The young of an insect or other animal that will change its form when it becomes an adult.

microscopic Too small to see without a microscope.

nocturnal Active at night. Many city creatures are nocturnal.

parasite A creature that lives on and feeds from another living thing.

pneumonia A serious disease of the lungs.

prey A creature hunted as food.

pupa The stage in an insect's life between larva and adult.

scavenger A creature that eats dead things.

species A group of animals or plants that look alike, behave in the same way and produce young that do the same.

stagnant water Still or stale water, as in a pond or ditch, that has no current to refresh it.

starvation Lack of food, often causing death.

sterilise To remove the ability of an animal to produce offspring.

tropics The hottest part of the world, near the equator.

urban Belonging to a town.

Index